**Quick Start Guides**

The New
AIR FRYER
Cookbook

Quick And Easy Air Fryer Recipes For Beginners.

Delicious Everyday Meals Anyone Can Cook.

First published in 2022 by Erin Rose Publishing

Text and illustration copyright © 2022 Erin Rose Publishing

Design: Julie Anson

DISCLAIMER: This book is for informational purposes only and not intended as a substitute for the medical advice, diagnosis or treatment of a physician or qualified healthcare provider. The reader should consult a physician before undertaking a new health care regime and in all matters relating to his/her health, and particularly with respect to any symptoms that may require diagnosis or medical attention.

While every care has been taken in compiling the recipes for this book we cannot accept responsibility for any problems which arise as a result of preparing one of the recipes. The author and publisher disclaim responsibility for any adverse effects that may arise from the use or application of the recipes in this book. Some of the recipes in this book include nuts and other allergens. If you have an allergy it's important to avoid these.

CONTENTS

AIR FRYER RECIPES

AIR FRYER BREAKFAST RECIPES

AIR FRYER LUNCH RECIPES

AIR FRYER DINNER RECIPES

Introduction

Not sure how to start cooking with your air fryer? You are not alone, but you will be able to get started straight away with this easy-to-use recipe book. You can begin cooking a diverse range of foods and delicious low fat meals quickly and economically.

You can discover how to make eggs exactly how you like them, plus tasty soups, casseroles, crispy fries, one-pot meals and cakes, you didn't know were possible to cook in an air fryer. Plus it reduces your need for other kitchen appliances. An air fryer has already replaced the microwave oven in many kitchens, as it's a healthier alternative to microwave cooking which only takes up a similar amount of counter space.

Frozen and fresh food cooked in the air fryer is crispy, delicious and effortless, so even if you're in a rush, you can still enjoy tasty breakfasts, lunches, dinners, side dishes and desserts in super quick time.

Cooking with an air fryer is one of the cheapest, easiest and healthiest ways to cook! The popularity of air frying is rocketing as more of us discover the advantages of the latest rapid air technology, to fry, roast, grill and bake.

By air frying you can enjoy crispy, tasty, lower fat meals in a less time, and you won't waste energy heating up your normal oven. It saves you money AND time to cook the most delicious food in the convenience of your air fryer.

In this calorie counted recipe book you will find plenty of tasty recipes which are super easy to cook and often take just a few minutes. You'll be happy to know, an air fryer even reduces your washing up which is a real bonus.

So, if you'd like to quickly get started using your new air fryer, or if you're already experienced and are looking for new and exciting recipes, look no further! This handy air fryer recipe book provides you with everything you need.

So whether you are cooking for one person or cooking for a family, there are recipes in this Quick Start Guide everyone will enjoy. Let's get started.

The Advantages of Using An Air Fryer

An air fryer is a smaller version of a convection or fan-assisted oven which is compact, easy-to-use and more economical than a traditional oven. It's not so much a 'fryer' in the usual sense. The air fryer has a heating element and the fan blows hot air inside the appliance so it cooks evenly and quickly using little or no oil.

A major benefit of cooking this way is that food becomes crispy on the outside while remaining tender on the inside. Food can be placed on trays or into the basket included and it also operates much like a grill at the top while hot air circulates and cooks the food evenly.

Air frying is a much healthier option than deep fat frying which involves re-heating the cooking oil which makes it toxic, and has been linked with various types of inflammatory illnesses and cancer.

You can choose what type of oils to use; avocado and light olive oil are two of the favourites. Oils begin to smoke at different temperatures, with avocado oil having a high smoke point, it can be used at higher temperatures, whereas olive oil has a lower smoke point so it's better for lower temperatures. Light olive oil is a great option, as it is healthy and has a higher smoke point than extra virgin olive oil but you can also use other vegetable oils or in some cases, you may want to ditch the oil altogether.

Getting to know your air fryer is important, especially when it comes to adding oil to food as some fryers are non stick and don't require oil whereas others do require oil to be added to the trays or basket, so check your instruction manual.

Using a spray bottle for your oil is ideal as it allows you to put a lighter coating of oil onto food. Also, some air fryers require some pre-heating so check the manual which comes with your air fryer.

As air fryers come in different sizes, starting from around 3 litres, some are only suitable for small portions or cooking for one, while others are more family orientated with more cooking space. Some have rotisserie features which are particularly handy. In this book we offer recipes for everyone and the portions can be multiplied or divided depending on your type of air fryer and number of people you are cooking for.

Once you have experimented with your air fryer a few times, you'll become more confident with the timers and functions. With most offering settings for various foods and pre-set temperatures although you can also set these yourself, especially if you are reheating foods.

Air fryers are a great way to save money on energy because not only do they use less electricity than a conventional oven but they cook more quickly as they are smaller and require less cooking time than large, traditional ovens, so, you are sure to save money on your energy bills.

Getting Started

Depending on your model of air fryer it will have a basket, drip tray and many models have shelves with some also having wire shelves, where food can be placed, so it varies between appliances. Having more space, especially shelves, will allow you to cook bigger quantities.

Any cookware such as bowls, plates and dishes which say they are 'oven proof' should be safe to use, and these could be made from aluminum, silicon, ceramic and glass. Air fryer accessories like liners, rotisserie skewers, pizza pans, tins, toast racks and egg molds are also available so you can invest in kitchenware made especially for an air fryer but if you don't wish to go to any expense you should be able to use some of your existing dishes, tins and smaller trays.

Please note, plastic could melt in your air fryer so don't to use it. Also, even though paper kitchen towels can be useful for wiping down the inside of your air fryer, it should not be left in or used during the cooking process, as this can become stuck in the top of the appliance, so make sure not to leave any remnants of paper towels you may have used during preparation or cleaning.

Whatever you place inside your air fryer, make sure not to block any air vents and always allow room for ventilation around the appliance on your countertop.

For marinating food in herbs, spices and oils you can use a bowl or even a zip-lock plastic bag to coat it well before cooking.

Essential Tips For Air Frying

Air fryers are great for warming leftovers and add crispness to foods which you don't get when you warm foods in a microwave. You can add a little spray of water or cooking oil to foods so they don't dry out too much. Always make sure food is thoroughly heated before you eat it. Usually setting the temperature to 180C/360F for will be the ideal setting for reheating or warming foods and the duration will vary according to the type of food and air fryer model.

When cooking frozen foods like chicken nuggets, battered fish, onion rings, fries, etc, remember that they may need less cooking time in the air fryer than the guidelines on the package suggest. Therefore, it's a good idea to set the timer for around ½ the suggested cooking time, flip it over and continue cooking to ¾ of the suggested time then check if it is done before allowing further cooking time if necessary.

When chopping foods, try to ensure they are the same size so the foods cooks evenly.

Very light foods can blow about during cooking due to it being a fan oven, so in this instance you can use some foil, a wire rack, or a toothpick to weigh it down. Things like dry oats blowing around inside your air fryer can make a real mess.

Lining the basket of your air fryer with foil or liners will prevent drips and reduce washing up. Be careful of parchment paper and never pre heat the air fryer with parchment paper inside it, as it can blow around and become stuck in the top.

Experiment with your favourite dishes and find the cooking times that work best for your model of air fryer and also your taste buds when it comes to crispness of your food. With foods which may not require much cooking time or that can dry out or become over done quickly, using 1 minute increments of cooking time will help you to work out how much cooking is required.

AIR FRYER BREAKFAST RECIPES

Air Fryer French Toast & Strawberries

Ingredients

- 10 strawberries, hulled and halved
- 4 slices thick white bread
- 2 eggs
- 1 teaspoon vanilla extract
- 1/2 teaspoon cinnamon
- 2 teaspoons honey

SERVES 2

261 calories per serving

Method

In a large bowl, whisk together the eggs, vanilla extract and cinnamon. Spray the air fryer basket liberally with cooking oil. Dip each slice of bread in the egg mixture and let any excess fall off. Lay the bread in the air fryer, making sure it isn't overlapping, and remember it may be best to cook it in batches. Cook in the air fryer at 200C/400F for 4 minutes then turn it over and continue cooking for another 4 minutes, or until the egg has set and the toast is golden. Serve with a drizzle of honey and a scattering of strawberries on top. Delicious!

Air Fryer Cheesy Omelette

Ingredients

- 25g (1oz) Cheddar cheese, grated (shredded)
- 2 large eggs
- 1 slice ham, chopped
- A small bunch of fresh basil, chopped

SERVES 1

271 calories per serving

Method

Preheat the air fryer to 160C/320F. Crack the eggs into a bowl and whisk them together. Add in the ham and cheese. Grease a small round oven-proof dish and pour in the eggs. Cook for 10 minutes and check to see if the mixture has set. It should be firm and not runny. Cook at 1 minute increments until it is completely cooked. Sprinkle with basil before serving. Enjoy.

Air Fryer Scrambled Eggs

Ingredients

- 4 large eggs
- 1 teaspoon butter
- Sea salt
- Black Pepper

SERVES 2

171 calories per serving

Method

Preheat your air fryer to 150C/300F. Crack the eggs into a bowl and whisk them together. Add in the butter and season with salt and pepper. Grease a small non-stick cake tin and pour in the egg mixture. Place them in the air fryer for 2 minutes. Stir the eggs then cook them for another 2 minutes. Stir and cook them again for 1 minute. Continue cooking them at 1 minute intervals until they are done to your liking, stirring frequently.

Air Fryer Poached Eggs

SERVES 4

134
calories
per serving

Method

Preheat the air fryer to 160C/320F. Take 4 ramekin dishes and quarter-fill them with warm water. Crack an egg into each ramekin dish. Transfer them to the air fryer and cook them for 5 minutes. Run a knife between the edge of the dish and the egg to dislodge it from the side. Cook for another 1-2 minutes until they are cooked to your liking. Strain off the water and serve.

Air Fryer Hard Boiled Eggs

Ingredients

4 medium eggs

SERVES 2

134
calories
per serving

Method

Preheat the air fryer to 120C/240F. Place the eggs into the basket of the air fryer and cook them for 15 minutes. When they are cooked, remove the eggs and place them into a bowl of cold water until they have cooled.

Air Fryer Crispy Bacon

Ingredients

4 slices of back bacon

SERVES 4

144
calories
per serving

Method

Preheat the air fryer to 180C/360F. Place the bacon onto a rack and make sure there is a drip tray in place at the bottom of the air fryer. You can also cook the bacon on parchment paper, although cooking on a rack will make it crispier. Cook for around 5 minutes then turn it over and continue cooking for another 5 minutes, or longer if you want it crispier.

Air Fryer Toast

Ingredients

2 slices of thick whole meal bread, (or whatever bread you prefer)

SERVES 1

204
calories
per serving

Method

Place the slices of bread into the air fryer in one layer, without them touching. Cook at 180C/360F for 4-5 minutes, or until the toast is golden and done to your liking. You can cook the toast in batches and keep warm if you are cooking for more people. Top with eggs, avocado, butter, jam, peanut butter or your favourite spread.

Air Fryer Sausages Wrapped In Bacon

Ingredients

4 large pork sausages

2 strips of smoky bacon, halved

2 dessert spoon maple syrup (or honey)

1/4 teaspoon cayenne pepper

SERVES 2

309 calories per serving

Method

Preheat the air fryer to 180C/360F. In a small bowl, mix together the cayenne pepper and maple syrup (or honey) then set it aside. Wind a piece of bacon around each sausage, wrapping it well. Coat each wrapped sausage with some of the maple syrup. Lay the sausages wrapped in bacon out in the air fryer in one single layer with enough space around them for the air to circulate. Cook them for 8 minutes then turn them over and continue cooking for a further 8 minutes. Make sure they are hot and cooked through before serving. Cooking time will vary depending on the thickness of the sausages and model of your air fryer.

Air Fryer Breakfast Frittata

Ingredients

- 50g (2oz) feta cheese, chopped
- 25g (1oz) Cheddar cheese, grated (shredded)
- 4 large eggs
- 2 spring onions (scallions), chopped
- 1 medium tomato, deseeded and chopped
- 1 small handful of fresh basil or parsley, chopped
- 1 large handful of fresh spinach, chopped
- 2 tablespoons whole milk
- Sea salt
- Freshly ground black pepper

SERVES 2

288 calories per serving

Method

Whisk together the eggs and the milk then add in the remaining ingredients. Season with salt and pepper. Preheat the air fryer to 180C/360F. Line a 20cm round spring-form tin with parchment paper and lightly grease it. Pour the egg mixture into the tin. Place it into the air fryer and cook for 12 minutes then check to see if it has completely set. Continue cooking for another 3-4 minutes if needed until it is completely cooked. Allow it to cook slightly then remove it from then tin and slice it before serving.

Air Fryer Bacon & Egg Breakfast Muffins

Ingredients

- 4 medium eggs
- 2 slices of bacon, chopped
- 1 tablespoon double cream (heavy cream) (or milk)
- 1 teaspoon olive oil
- 1/4 teaspoon garlic powder
- 1/4 teaspoon mixed herbs
- Sea salt
- Freshly ground black pepper

SERVES 2

303 calories per serving

Method

Place the bacon into the air fryer and cook for 4 minutes then turn it over and cook for another 4 minutes or until it is completely cooked. Roughly chop the bacon. In a bowl, whisk together the eggs then add in the garlic, cream, mixed herbs, bacon and season with salt and pepper. Lightly grease a muffin tin with olive oil then pour some mixture into 4 of the cups. Cook at 150C/300F for around 12 minutes before checking to see if the bacon and egg muffins have set. Enjoy straight away.

AIR FRYER LUNCH RECIPES

Air Fryer Cheesy Quesadillas

Ingredients

- 75g (3oz) Cheddar cheese, grated, (shredded)
- 4 soft whole wheat tortillas
- 1 ripe avocado, flesh only, mashed
- Sea salt
- Freshly ground black pepper

SERVES 4

252
calories
per serving

Method

Preheat the air fryer to 180C/360F. Spread the mashed avocado over half of both the tortillas. Scatter on the cheese and season with salt and pepper. Fold the tortillas in half, pressing the edges together. Place the tortillas into the air fryer and cook for 2 minutes. Check they are still closed and cook for 2 minutes. The cheese should have melted and be piping hot.

Air Fryer Baked Brie & Cranberries

Ingredients

SERVES 4

432 calories per serving

- 25g (1oz) dried cranberries, chopped
- 25g (1oz) walnuts, chopped
- 1 round brie (approx 200g/7oz)
- 1 tablespoon honey

Method

Trim off just the top rind of the brie, leaving the bottom and sides intact. Place it on an ovenproof dish which fits inside the air fryer. Place it in the air fryer and cook at 180C/360F for around 6 minutes or until the cheese is soft. In the meantime, warm the honey in a microwave or small saucepan and stir in the cranberries and walnuts. Spoon the mixture on top of the brie. Serve with crusty bread, crackers, sourdough bread or apple & celery slices.

Air Fryer Halloumi & Apple Slices

Ingredients

1 block of halloumi, drained and sliced

2 large apples, cored and sliced

Sprinkling of cinnamon

SERVES 2

335 calories per serving

Method

Preheat the air fryer to 180C/360F. Place the apple slices on a wire shelf and cook them for 5 minutes. Place the halloumi slices on another shelf and place it in the top part of the air fryer along with the apple on a lower shelf. Cook for around 5 minutes or until golden. Serve the apple with a sprinkling of cinnamon and add the halloumi on top. Eat straight away. Delicious for breakfast, lunch or a snack.

Air Fryer Mozzarella Sticks

Ingredients

- 200g (7oz) mozzarella ball
- 25g (1oz) panko breadcrumbs
- 1 medium egg
- 1 tablespoon plain (all-purpose) flour
- ½ teaspoon garlic powder

SERVES 2

357 calories per serving

Method

Drain off any liquid from the mozzarella and cut it into strips just over 1cm (½ inch) wide. Place the flour and garlic powder into a dish and place the breadcrumbs in a separate dish. Crack the egg into a bowl, add some salt and pepper and beat it well. Coat the mozzarella in the flour mixture, dip it in the egg, and then back to the flour again for another dip, making sure the strips are completely coated. Coat the mozzarella in the breadcrumbs. Lay it on a plate and transfer it to the freezer for around 40 minutes to firm up. Spray the air fryer basket with oil and place the mozzarella sticks in it, making sure they aren't touching. Add a spray of oil to them. Cook in the air fryer for around 10 minutes at 200C/400F. You may wish to cook them in batches and warm them for a minute or so before serving if necessary.

Air Fryer Bacon & Avocado Wedges With Garlic Mayo

Ingredients

SERVES 4

291 calories per serving

- 8 slices of streaky bacon, halved lengthwise
- 2 ripe avocados
- 2 tablespoons mayonnaise
- 2 cloves of garlic, peeled and crushed
- Squeeze of lemon juice (optional)

Method

Cut the avocados in half and remove the stone and skin. Cut each avocado half into quarters. Wrap a piece of bacon around each piece of avocado. Lay the avocado pieces into the air fryer, allowing room for the air to flow. Cook for 7 minutes then turn them over and continue cooking for another 7 minutes. The bacon should be golden. Mix the mayonnaise with the garlic and a squeeze of lemon juice and stir well. Serve the bacon and avocado with the garlic mayo and enjoy!

Air Fryer Ham & Goat's Cheese Pastries

Ingredients

225g (8oz) goats' cheese

4 slices of ham, chopped

1 sheet of puff pastry

MAKES 16

104 calories per serving

Method

Preheat the air fryer to 180C/360F. Lightly flour a flat surface and roll out the puff pastry into a square shape and cut it in 16 pieces. Add some ham to the middle of each piece of pastry and add some cheese on top. Take 2 opposite corners and bring them together. Overlap them slightly and press the edges together to make a semi rolled up shape. Place them on the lightly greased shelves or basket of the air fryer. Cook them for 10-12 minutes or until the pastry is golden.

Air Fryer Tomato Soup

Ingredients

- 6 tomatoes, halved
- 3 cloves of garlic, peeled and chopped
- 1 onion, peeled and roughly chopped
- 1 teaspoon sugar (optional)
- A handful of fresh basil, chopped
- 475mls (16fl oz) chicken stock (broth)
- 75mls (3 fl oz) double cream (heavy cream)
- 1 tablespoon olive oil
- Sea salt
- Freshly ground black pepper

SERVES 2

322 calories per serving

Method

Line the basket of the air fryer with foil or parchment paper. Place the onion, tomatoes, garlic, olive oil and sugar (if using) into a bowl and coat the vegetables in the oil. Season with salt and pepper. Transfer them to the basket of the air fryer and cook at 200C/400F for 10 minutes. Flip the vegetables around, then cook them for another 10 minutes or until the vegetables are soft. Transfer the vegetables to a food processor and blend until smooth. Pour the mixture into a large saucepan, add the chicken stock (broth) and cream and warm it through. Serve with a sprinkle of fresh basil and enjoy!

Air Fryer Butternut Squash Soup

Ingredients

- 1 butternut squash, peeled, chopped into 2cm (1 inch) chunks
- 1 onion, cut into wedges
- 4 cloves of garlic peeled and chopped
- 1/4 teaspoon chilli powder
- 1/4 teaspoon smoked paprika
- A small handful of fresh thyme or coriander (cilantro)
- 950mls (2 pints) vegetable or chicken stock (broth)
- 2 tablespoons olive oil
- Sea salt

SERVES 4

170 calories per serving

Method

Place the oil, chilli powder and garlic into a bowl and mix well. Add the squash, carrot and onion and toss them in the oil. Season with salt. Transfer the vegetables it to the air fryer and cook at 200C/400F for 15 minutes. Toss it around and cook for another 15 minutes or until the vegetables are soft. Place the vegetables into a food processor and blitz until smooth. Add the paprika and fresh herbs. Pour the soup into a saucepan and add in the stock (broth). Heat it until it's warm. Serve and enjoy.

Air Fryer Hot Dogs

Ingredients

4 thick pork sausages

4 hot dog rolls

1 onion, peeled and thinly sliced

SERVES 4

308 calories per serving

Method

Prick the sausages and lay them in the basket of the air fryer. Cook at 200C/400F for 6 minutes then turn them over. Press your thumb into the onion slices to make rings and add them to the air fryer. Cook for 6 minutes. Check to see if the sausages are cooked through and add extra cooking time if you need to. Slice the hot dog rolls and place a sausage inside each one and add some onion on top. Place it in the air fryer and cook for 1 minute to warm the rolls. Serve with your favourite condiment, pickles, coleslaw or relish.

Air Fryer Cajun Chicken Drumsticks

Ingredients

- 12 chicken drumsticks
- 1 teaspoon paprika
- 1 teaspoon garlic powder
- 1/4 teaspoon thyme
- 1/4 teaspoon oregano
- 1/4 teaspoon chilli powder
- 1 tablespoon olive oil

SERVES 4

346 calories per serving

Method

Preheat the air fryer to 200C/400F. Place all the seasonings and oil into a bowl and mix them well. Add the chicken drumsticks and coat them well in the mixture. Place the chicken drumsticks into the air fryer in one layer, bearing in mind you may need to cook them in batches if it's a small capacity air fryer. Cook them for 12 minutes then flip them over. Continue cooking for another 12 minutes and check if they are done using a meat thermometer. Add extra cooking time if you need to. Remove them and serve. These go great with coleslaw, salads and are so versatile plus they're a kid's favourite.

Air Fryer French Bread Pizza

Ingredients

- 75g (3oz) mozzarella cheese, grated
- 14 slices of pepperoni
- 2 tablespoons passata/tomato sauce
- ½ French baguette
- Mixed herbs or Italian seasoning

SERVES 2

524
calories
per serving

Method

Preheat the air fryer to 190C/380F. Slice the French bread lengthwise. Cut the bread to a width which fits into your air fryer. Spoon the tomato sauce on the bread and spread it out. Sprinkle the cheese on top and add the pepperoni slices. Place it in the air fryer and cook for 5 minutes until the cheese has melted and the bread is warm and crisp. Serve and eat straight away.

Air Fryer Falafel Wraps

Ingredients

2 large whole meal (or white) wraps

2 tomatoes, sliced

1 tablespoon houmous

1 small chilli, deseeded and chopped

½ onion, peeled and sliced

½ red pepper (bell pepper), deseeded and finely chopped

FOR THE FALAFEL

400g (14oz) tin chickpeas, drained

2 cloves of garlic, peeled and roughly chopped

1 small handful of fresh coriander (cilantro)

Zest of ½ lemon

½ small onion, peeled and chopped

½ teaspoon ground coriander (cilantro)

½ teaspoon sea salt

2 tablespoons water

SERVES 2

467 calories per serving

Method

Preheat the air fryer to 200°C. Place all the ingredients for the falafels into a food processor and blitz until the mixture sticks together. You can add an extra tablespoon of water to the mixture if it seems too dry. Shape the mixture into 8 balls. Spray a little vegetable oil into the basket of the air fryer and lay the falafels out in a single layer. Cook at 200C/400F for around 15 minutes or until crisp and golden. Lay out the flat breads/naan bread and spread houmous on top. Place some falafels on top. Sprinkle the tomatoes, onion and chill (if using) on top and wrap it. Serve while the falafels are still warm. Enjoy. You can experiment with different fillings, like guacamole, sour cream, sweet chilli or yogurt dip.

Air Fryer Garlic Mushrooms

Ingredients

- 300g (11oz) medium sized mushrooms, halved
- 3 cloves of garlic, peeled and chopped
- 1 teaspoon garlic powder
- 1 teaspoon soy sauce
- 1 teaspoon olive oil
- ½ teaspoon pepper
- Small bunch of fresh parsley, chopped

SERVES 2

39 calories per serving

Method

Preheat the air fryer to 190C/380F. Place the mushrooms, soy sauce, olive oil pepper, garlic and garlic powder into a bowl and mix well. Place the mushrooms in an oven proof dish and transfer them to the air fryer. Cook for 5 minutes and flip them over. Cook for 3-5 minutes. Sprinkle the freshly chopped parsley on top. Serve with toast, pasta, tortilla, crusty bread or salad.

Air Fryer Courgette Fries

Ingredients

- 50g (2oz) panko breadcrumbs
- 2 medium courgettes (zucchini)
- 1 egg
- 1 tablespoon Parmesan cheese, grated (shredded)
- 1 teaspoon onion powder
- 1 teaspoon garlic powder
- ½ teaspoon sea salt
- ½ teaspoon black pepper

SERVES 2

175
calories
per serving

Method

Cut the courgettes (zucchini) in half then into lengthways strips of around 1 cm (½ inch) thick so they look like fries. Crack the egg into a bowl and beat it. Place the breadcrumbs, onion, garlic, salt, pepper and Parmesan into a bowl and mix well. Dip the courgette pieces into the egg then into the dry mixture. Lightly spray the air fryer basket with cooking oil. Place them into the air fryer basket and give the fries a little spray of oil. Cook at 200C/400F for 6 minutes then check if they are cooked. Cook for another 2-3 minutes if you need to. Enjoy as they are or serve with garlic mayonnaise, sour cream dip, salsa or guacamole.

Air Fryer Turkey Burgers

Ingredients

- 450g (1lb) minced (ground) turkey
- 4 burger baps, halved
- 4 lettuce leaves
- 2 tomatoes, sliced
- 1 egg, beaten
- ½ onion, peeled and very finely chopped
- 1 teaspoon balsamic vinegar
- Sea salt
- Freshly ground black pepper

SERVES 4

318 calories per serving

Method

Place all of the ingredients into a large bowl and mix them well. Season with salt and pepper. Divide the mixture into 4 and shape it into 4 balls then flatten them into a round shape. Place each burger into the air fryer with enough space between them to allow the air to circulate. Make sure the drip tray is in place at the bottom to catch any liquid. Cook at 200C/400F for 6 minutes. Turn the burgers over and cook them for another 6 minutes. Place some lettuce into each burger bun and add the burger with some tomato on top. Enjoy.

Air Fryer
Goats Cheese Balls

Ingredients

200g (7oz) goats' cheese

50g (2oz) panko breadcrumbs

2 tablespoons plain flour

1 egg

1 tablespoon honey

2 large handfuls of green salad leaves

**SERVES
2**

564
calories
per serving

Method

Separate the goats' cheese into 20 equal portions and roll them into balls. Crack the egg into a bowl and whisk it. Place the flour in one bowl and the breadcrumbs into another bowl. Dip each piece of goats' cheese in the egg, then the flour and then the breadcrumbs. Spray some cooking oil onto the air fryer basket. Transfer them to the air fryer and give them a spray of cooking oil. Cook at 190C/380F for 4 minutes then turn them over and cook for another 2 minutes or until golden. Serve with the salad leaves and a drizzle of honey. Enjoy!

Air Fryer Goats' Cheese & Sweet Potato Pittas

Ingredients

- 100g (3oz) goats' cheese
- 2 whole meal pitta bread
- 1 cooked sweet potato (leftovers are ideal), diced
- 1 teaspoon olive oil
- A small bunch of basil, chopped
- Sea salt
- Freshly ground black pepper

SERVES 2

392 calories per serving

Method

Scatter the sweet potato and goats' cheese on top of the pitta bread. Season with salt and pepper. Add a drizzle of olive oil and place it in the air fryer. Cook at 200C/400F for 4-6 minutes, or until the cheese has melted. Sprinkle with basil and serve.

Air Fryer Honey Roast Carrot & Feta Salad

Ingredients

- 250g (9oz) carrots, peeled and cut into strips
- 150g (5oz) feta cheese, chopped
- 50g (2oz) dried cranberries, chopped
- 1 Cos lettuce, chopped
- ½ teaspoon dried mixed herbs
- 1 tablespoon olive oil

SERVES 2

377
calories
per serving

Method

Place the oil and mixed herbs in a bowl and coat the carrots in the mixture. Transfer them to an ovenproof dish that fits in your air fryer and cook at 190C/380F for around 5 minutes. Flip them around and continue cooking for another 3-5 minutes or until they have softened. Scatter the feta cheese and honey on top. Return it to the air fryer and cook for around 2 minutes or until the cheese is warm. Serve with some lettuce and a sprinkling of dried cranberries. Enjoy straight away.

AIR FRYER
DINNER
RECIPES

Air Fryer Salmon with Balsamic & Ginger

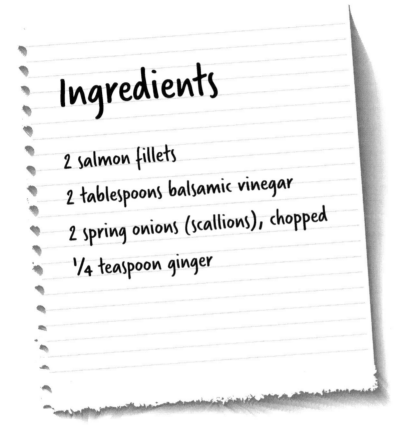

Ingredients

- 2 salmon fillets
- 2 tablespoons balsamic vinegar
- 2 spring onions (scallions), chopped
- 1/4 teaspoon ginger

SERVES 2

304 calories per serving

Method

Preheat the air fryer to 200C/400F. Place the salmon, balsamic and ginger into a bowl or plastic bag and allow it to marinate for at least 30 minutes. Line the bottom of the air fryer basket with parchment or foil. Lay the salmon fillets in the basket. Cook for 8 minutes and check if it is opaque. Continue cooking for 1 minute increments until it is completely cooked. Serve with a sprinkling of spring onions (scallions). Enjoy.

Air Fryer Bang Bang Prawns

Ingredients

50g (2oz) panko breadcrumbs

14 jumbo prawns (shrimp)

1 egg, beaten

BANG BANG SAUCE:

3 tablespoons mayonnaise

1 clove of garlic, peeled and chopped

½ teaspoon Tabasco sauce (or Sriracha)

1 tablespoon ketchup

SERVES 2

342
calories
per serving

Method

Preheat the air fryer to 200C/400F. Dip the prawns (shrimp) in the beaten egg and then dip and coat them in the breadcrumbs. Spray the basket of the air fryer with a little oil. Lay the prawns (shrimp) in the basket, spacing them out for the air to flow around them. Lightly spray some oil onto the prawns. Cook them for 3 minutes then turn them over and cook for another 3 minutes. Check that they are crisp and completely cooked.

Mix together all of the ingredients for the bang bang sauce and add extra hot sauce if required. Serve with the prawns (shrimp). Enjoy!

Air Fryer
Steak & Mushrooms

Ingredients

- 200g (7oz) mushrooms, sliced
- 2 beef rump steaks, (approx 450g/1lb, sliced)
- 1 tablespoon Worcestershire sauce
- 1 teaspoon paprika
- 1 tablespoon olive oil
- Sea salt
- Black pepper

SERVES 4

547 calories per serving

Method

Place the oil, paprika and Worcestershire sauce into a bowl and stir well. Add the beef and mushrooms to the bowl and coat them in the oil mixture. Season with salt and pepper. If you have time you can marinade it for an hour or so. Preheat the air fryer to 200C/400F. Cook for around 3-4 minutes then flip the steak. Continue cooking for another 3-4 minutes or until the steak is cooked how you like it. Serve and enjoy.

Air Fryer Cauliflower Buffalo Wings

Ingredients

- 125g (4oz) plain flour
- 2 tablespoons buffalo sauce or chilli sauce
- 1 cauliflower, broken into florets around 5cm (2 inches)
- 1 teaspoon baking powder
- 150mls (¼ pint) cold water
- Spray of vegetable oil
- Sea salt
- Freshly ground black pepper

SERVES 4

166 calories per serving

Method

Preheat the air fryer to 200C. Place the baking powder and flour into a bowl and add some salt and pepper. Gradually whisk the water into the flour mixture until it becomes smooth. Add the cauliflower pieces and coat them in the batter mixture. Coat the air fryer basket with a spray of oil. Spread the cauliflower pieces out in a single layer and spray them with a little more oil. Cook for around 10 minutes, or until they are crisp and golden. You may wish to cook them in batches to make sure they cook evenly. You can return the first batch to the air fryer to warm them just before serving. Serve with a dollop of buffalo sauce on the side or in a small dish. Enjoy.

Air Fryer Homemade Cheese Burgers

Ingredients

- 450g (1lb) minced beef (ground beef)
- 4 burger baps, sliced
- 4 slices of Cheddar cheese
- 4 small lettuce leaves
- 2 medium tomatoes, sliced
- 1 onion, peeled and thinly sliced
- ¼ teaspoon onion powder
- ¼ teaspoon garlic powder
- ¼ teaspoon sea salt
- ¼ teaspoon black pepper

SERVES 4

451
calories
per serving

Method

Preheat the air fryer to 190C/380F. Place the beef, onion powder, garlic powder, sea salt and black pepper into a large bowl and using clean hands, combine the mixture. Shape them into 4 equal sized balls then flatten them. Press your finger into the middle to make a slight indentation. Lay the burgers into the air fryer and cook them for 5 minutes. Turn them over and continue cooking for a further 5 minutes. Check that they are completely cooked through and allow a few minutes extra cooking time if they are not completely cooked. You can use a meat thermometer to double check. Place a slice of cheese on each burger and warm them in the air fryer for 1 minute. Place some lettuce and onion into each burger bun then add the burger and tomato slices. Enjoy!

Air Fryer Satay Chicken

Ingredients

- 450g (1lb) chicken breast
- 1 teaspoon turmeric
- 1 teaspoon cumin
- 1 teaspoon ground coriander (cilantro)
- ½ teaspoon pepper
- 2 tablespoons soy sauce
- 4 tablespoons thick coconut milk (or coconut cream)
- 2 teaspoons grated (shredded) ginger root

SERVES 4

207
calories
per serving

Method

Preheat the air fryer to 190C/380F. Place all of the ingredients into a bowl and marinate the chicken for at least an hour or overnight if you can. Spray the air fryer basket with a little oil. Place the chicken into the basket laying it out in a single layer to ensure even cooking – you may need to do 2 batches, depending on the size of your fryer. Cook for 14 minutes then turn it over and cook for around 10 minutes or until completely opaque and cooked through. Serve with rice or a heap of salad.

Air Fryer
Texan Style Beef Ribs

Ingredients

- 2 beef short ribs (edible portion, approx 100g (3½oz each)
- 3 teaspoons sweet paprika
- 2 teaspoons ground cumin
- 2 teaspoons garlic powder
- 2 teaspoons onion powder
- 1 teaspoon ground black pepper
- 1 teaspoon sea salt
- 1 tablespoon olive oil

SERVES 2

296
calories
per serving

Method

Preheat the air fryer to 200C/400F. Place all of the rub ingredients into a bowl and mix them really well. Coat the ribs thoroughly in the mixture. Transfer the ribs to the air fryer and cook them for around 10 minutes. Turn the ribs over and reduce the heat to 160C/320F and cook for 20 minutes. Use a meat thermometer to check if the ribs are thoroughly cooked. You can continue cooking for 1-2 minute intervals if they are thick and need longer cooking time. This recipe doesn't contain any added sugar, but if you wish to add barbeque sauce you can coat the ribs in it towards the end of cooking.

Air Fryer Roast Chicken

Ingredients

- 1 whole chicken
- 2 teaspoons paprika
- ½ teaspoon mixed herbs
- ½ teaspoon sea salt
- 2 teaspoons light olive oil (or avocado oil)

SERVES 4

393 calories per serving

Method

Firstly, choose a chicken that fits easily into your air fryer that allows plenty of room for the air to circulate around the appliance. It can be placed in the basket or some air fryers have a rotisserie function for this purpose.

Preheat the air fryer to 180C/360F. In a bowl, mix together the olive oil, paprika, herbs and salt then rub the mixture into the chicken skin. Place the chicken into the air fryer basket breast side down. Cook for 45 minutes then turn the chicken over so that it is breast side up. Continue cooking for 10-15 minutes. Using a meat thermometer, check to see if it has completely cooked at the thickest part of the chicken. Return it to the air fryer and continue cooking for another 5 minutes or longer if it needed.

Air Fryer Honey & Mustard Sausage One-Pot

Ingredients

- 350g (12oz) baby potatoes
- 6 pork sausages
- 2 teaspoons wholegrain mustard
- 1 onion, peeled and chopped
- 1 tablespoon light olive oil
- 2 teaspoons honey
- 1 red pepper (bell pepper), deseeded and chopped

SERVES 2

552 calories per serving

Method

Preheat the air-fryer to 180C/360F. Chop the potatoes in half or smaller so that they are similar sizes. Place the potatoes, onion, olive oil into a bowl and season with salt and pepper. Transfer them to the air fryer and cook for around 10 minutes. In the meantime, stir together the mustard and honey then coat the sausages in the mixture. Add the sausages to the air-fryer and cook for 6 minutes. Flip the food in the air-fryer and add the peppers (bell peppers). Continue cooking for 7 minutes. Check that the sausages are thoroughly cooked and if you need to cook for a little longer in 1-2 minute increments until done. This is a delicious one-pot meal that you can try adding different vegetables, like tomatoes or asparagus and just give them a spray of cooking oil before adding them.

Air Fryer Loaded Potato Skins

Ingredients

125g (4oz) Cheddar cheese, grated (shredded)

4 cooked potatoes, halved

4 slices of cooked bacon, crumbled

4 spring onions (scallions), chopped

1 tablespoon olive oil

SERVES 4

408 calories per serving

Method

Scoop a little of the flesh of the potato out to make an indentation where the other ingredients will go. Coat the potatoes in a little olive oil and transfer them to the air fryer. Cook at 200C/400F for 5 minutes. In the meantime, in a bowl, mix together the leftover potato flesh, cheese, bacon and spring onions. Carefully remove the potatoes. Spoon some of the cheese mixture into each of the potato skins. Reduce the cooking temperature to 180C/360F. Return the potatoes to the air fryer and cook them for around 2 minutes or until they are warmed through and the cheese has melted. Serve on their own, with garlic butter or with a dollop of sour cream, ranch dressing or mayonnaise.

Air Fryer
Chicken Tikka Kebabs

Ingredients

75g (3oz) Tikka Massala paste (or spice powder)

2 large chicken breasts, diced

2 tablespoons plain (unflavoured) yogurt

2 cloves of garlic, finely chopped

1 tablespoon olive oil

Juice of ½ lemon

SERVES 2

428
calories
per serving

Method

If you don't have metal skewers for your air fryer you can use wooden skewers for this purpose, just soak them in water before you use them. You can also trim the wooden skewers to make them fit inside your air fryer. Place the yogurt, oil and spice paste into a bowl and mix well. Add the chicken pieces to the spicy yogurt mixture and coat it completely then allow it to marinate for at least an hour. Thread the meat onto the skewers. Spray the air fryer basket with a little oil. Transfer the skewers to the air fryer. Cook them at 180C/360F for 8 minutes then turn them. Continue cooking for around 7 minutes and check if they are completely cooked. You may want to use a meat thermometer for this purpose. When they are done, serve with rice, vegetable dishes or a side salad.

Air Fryer Chicken Wings & Sweet Chilli Sauce

Ingredients

- 700g (1.5lb) chicken wings
- 1 teaspoon sea salt
- 1 teaspoon garlic powder
- 1 teaspoon white pepper

CHILLI SAUCE:

- 2 cloves of garlic, peeled and chopped
- 1 red chilli, chopped
- 2 tablespoons honey
- 2 tablespoons lime juice
- 1 tablespoon sesame oil

SERVES 4

339 calories per serving

Method

Place the garlic powder, salt and pepper into a bowl and rub the mixture into the chicken wings. Spread the chicken wings into the basket of the air fryer, allowing room for the air to flow. Cook at 200C/400F for 25 minutes. Turn them over and continue cooking for another 10 minutes.

Mix together all of the ingredients for the chili sauce. When the chicken wings are completely cooked, drizzle the sweet chilli sauce over the top. Serve and enjoy.

Air Fryer Sea Bass, Asparagus & Lemon Dressing

Ingredients

- 10 asparagus spears
- 2 medium sea bass fillets
- 1 tablespoon olive oil
- Sea salt

FOR THE LEMON DRESSING:

- 2 teaspoons capers
- 1 teaspoon mustard
- 1½ tablespoon olive oil
- Zest and juice of ½ lemon
- Freshly chopped parsley to garnish

SERVES 2

317
calories
per serving

Method

Preheat the air-fryer to 180C/360F. Coat the asparagus and the fish with a little oil and season with salt and pepper. Place the asparagus into the air fryer and cook it for 3 minutes and then turn it. Add the fish to the air fryer and cook for 4-5 minutes. Use a meat thermometer and check that the fish is completely cooked. Cook a little longer if necessary. Place all the ingredients for the dressing into a small container and still well. Serve the fish and asparagus with the dressing and a sprinkle of fresh parsley. This goes well with a heap of salad, pasta or new potatoes.

Air Fryer Stuffed Peppers

Ingredients

- 400g (14oz) passata tomato sauce
- 400g (14oz) tin of kidney beans, drained
- 250g (9oz) pack of cooked rice
- 100g (3½ oz) mozzarella cheese
- 4 large red peppers (Bell Peppers), stalk and top removed
- 4 tomatoes, diced
- 1 teaspoon mixed herbs

SERVES 4

276 calories per serving

Method

Scoop out the seeds from the inside of the pepper. In a bowl combine the tomatoes, tomato sauce, rice, kidney beans and mixed herbs. Stuff the peppers with the mixture. Transfer them to the basket of the air fryer and cook at 180C/360F for around 12 minutes. Top them with the cheese and continue cooking until the cheese has melted. Eat straight away.

Air Fryer Chicken Fried Rice

Ingredients

- 400g (14oz) cooked white rice, (leftovers or pre-cooked packet)
- 225g (8oz) cooked chicken
- 75g (3oz) frozen peas
- 75g (3oz) frozen chopped carrots (or leftovers chopped)
- 3 spring onions (scallions), chopped
- 1 egg, beaten
- 5 tablespoons soy sauce
- 1 tablespoon olive oil

SERVES 2

603 calories per serving

Method

Place the olive oil and soy sauce into a large bowl and mix it well. Add in the chicken and rice and stir it well. Add in the peas and carrots and stir them through the mixture. Transfer the rice to an ovenproof dish and place it in the air fryer. Cook on 180C/360F for 10 minutes. Remove the rice and pour in the beaten egg, stirring it well through the mixture. Continue cooking for around another 5 minutes and stir again, breaking up the cooked egg. Cook for another 4-5 minutes or until the rice is completely warmed through. Serve with a sprinkling of spring onions (scallions) and eat straight away.

Air Fryer Breaded Garlic Chicken Breast

Ingredients

SERVES 4

288 calories per serving

- 75g (3oz) panko breadcrumbs (or other breadcrumbs)
- 4 chicken breasts, flattened
- 1 egg
- 1 teaspoon garlic powder
- 1/4 teaspoon sea salt
- Freshly ground black pepper

Method

In a bowl, combine the breadcrumbs, garlic, salt and pepper. In a separate bowl, crack the egg and beat it well. Dip the chicken breasts into the egg then dip it into the breadcrumbs mixture, making sure it is well coated. Put a piece of air fryer parchment paper into the air fryer basket to help prevent it from sticking. Cook at 190C/380F for around 10 minutes. Turn the chicken over onto the other side and continue cooking for around 5 minutes. Use a meat thermometer to check it is cooked through. You can add extra time of 1-2 minute intervals if it needs more cooking time. This is a great staple which can be enjoyed with salads, vegetables, pasta or fries.

Air Fryer Pork Chops

Ingredients

4 boneless, lean pork chops
(approx. 150g/5oz each)

½ teaspoon garlic powder

½ teaspoon onion powder

1 teaspoon olive oil

1 teaspoon smoked paprika

**SERVES
4**

290
calories
per serving

Method

Preheat the air fryer to 190C/380F. Place all of the ingredients into a large bowl and coat the chops in the oil and seasoning. Cook the pork chops in the air fryer for 5 minutes, then turn them over and continue cooking for a further 5 minutes. Depending on the thickness of the chops, check that they are cooked through. Cook for further 1 minute increments if they need it.

Air Fryer Sausage & Vegetable Casserole

Ingredients

- 100g (3½ oz) Brussels sprouts
- 4 pork sausages, cut into 2cm (1 inch) pieces
- 2 apples, peeled, cored and chopped
- 1 sweet potato, peeled and diced
- 1 onion, peeled and chopped
- 1 tablespoon olive oil
- 1 teaspoon dried thyme
- Sea salt
- Freshly ground black pepper

SERVES 2

465
calories
per serving

Method

Place the oil and thyme into a bowl and mix well. Add the sprouts, sweet potato and onion and coat them in the oil. Season with salt and pepper. Transfer them to the basket of the air fryer and cook at 180C/360F for 7 minutes. Flip the vegetables and scatter the sausage pieces on top. Cook for around 10 minutes. Sprinkle the apple pieces on top and continue cooking for 3 minutes until the apple has warmed and the sausages are completely cooked and golden. You can add some extra cooking time if you like your vegetables crispier. Serve and enjoy.

Air Fryer Aubergine & Mozzarella Gratin

Ingredients

200g (7oz) mozzarella, thinly sliced

25g (1oz) Parmesan cheese, grated (shredded)

1 large aubergine, sliced to ½ cm (¼ inch) thick

1 tablespoon olive oil

Sea salt

FOR THE TOMATO SAUCE:

150g (5oz) passata tomato sauce

1 teaspoon dried oregano

½ teaspoon garlic powder

1 tablespoon olive oil

A small bunch of fresh basil, chopped

SERVES 2

473 calories per serving

Method

Preheat the air-fryer to 200C/400F. Coat the aubergine (eggplant) with olive oil and a sprinkling of salt. Lay the aubergine (eggplant) flat in the air fryer – you may need to cook it in 2 batches. Cook for around 3 minutes then turn it over and cook for another 3 minutes. Lay some aubergine slices on the bottom of an ovenproof dish, which fits into your air fryer. In a small bowl, mix together the ingredients for the tomato sauce. Spoon the sauce over the aubergine. Lay slices of mozzarella on top. Add another layer of aubergine, followed by mozzarella and Parmesan. Place it in the air fryer and cook for 5-6 minutes or until it becomes golden. Serve with a heap of salad or vegetables.

Air Fryer
Turkey Pasta Bake

Ingredients

- 250g (9oz) passata or tomato pasta sauce
- 225g (8oz) minced (ground) turkey, (or other meat)
- 175g (6oz) whole wheat pasta shells
- 75g (3oz) mozzarella cheese, grated (shredded)
- 1 onion, peeled and chopped
- 1 red pepper (bell pepper), deseeded and chopped
- 1 tablespoon olive oil

SERVES 2

698 calories per serving

Method

Cook the pasta according to the instructions on the packet. When it has cooked drain it and set it aside. Heat the oil in a frying pan and add the onion and red pepper (bell pepper) and cook for 4 minutes. Add the minced (ground) turkey and brown the meat, stirring frequently. Stir in the passata/tomato sauce and the cooked pasta and mix well. Remove it from the heat. Transfer the mixture to an oven proof casserole dish which fits inside your air fryer. Sprinkle the top of the casserole with cheese. Cook at 180C/360F for 6-8 minutes, or until the cheese has melted and is gently bubbling.

Air Fryer Mexican Chicken Casserole

Ingredients

400g (14oz) tin of black beans, drained

400g (14oz) tin of chopped tomatoes

350g (12oz) tin of cream of chicken soup

75g (3oz) cheese, grated (shredded)

75g (3oz) tortilla chips, crushed

6 soft tortillas, torn into pieces

2 cooked chicken breasts, chopped

2 red chillies, deseeded and chopped

1 teaspoon cumin

1 tablespoon sour cream

1 bunch of fresh coriander (cilantro), chopped

SERVES 2

718 calories per serving

Method

Place the black beans, chicken, chicken soup, tomatoes, chillies and cumin into a bowl and mix well. Spray some oil into an ovenproof dish which fits inside your air fryer. Cover the bottom of the dish with HALF of the tortilla pieces. Spoon half of the chicken mixture on top. Top it with half of the grated (shredded) cheese. Layer the remaining tortilla pieces on top of the mixture followed by the remaining chicken mixture. Cover the casserole with foil and cook for around 40 minutes at 180C/360F. Remove the toil and sprinkle the crushed tortilla chips and cheese on top. Return it to the air fryer until the casserole is hot throughout and the cheesy tortilla topping has melted and golden. Serve with a dollop of sour cream and a sprinkle of fresh coriander (cilantro).

Air Fryer
Sweet & Sour Chicken

Ingredients

450g (1lb) chicken pieces, chopped into 3cm (1½ inch) chunks

2 tablespoons corn flour (cornstarch)

Sea salt

FOR THE SWEET & SOUR SAUCE

240mls (8 fl oz) pineapple juice

100g (3½ oz) brown sugar

3 tablespoons rice wine vinegar

1 tablespoon soy sauce

1 teaspoon freshly grated (shredded) ginger

2 tablespoons corn flour (cornstarch)

2 tablespoons water

SERVES 4

372 calories per serving

Method

Place the chicken and 2 tablespoons corn flour (cornstarch) into a bowl and coat it well. Season with a little salt. Spray the basket of the air fryer with vegetable oil. Place the chicken chunks into the air fryer in a single layer. Cook it at 200C/400F for around 4 minutes, then flip it around and continue cooking for another 4–5 minutes or until the chicken is completely cooked.

In the meantime, place the pineapple juice, sugar, rice wine vinegar, ginger and soy sauce into a saucepan and bring it to a gentle simmer, stirring frequently. Mix together the corn flour (cornstarch) and water until it becomes a smooth paste. Add the paste to the sweet and sour sauce, stirring well. Add in the pineapple chunks and warm it for around a minute. Add the chicken to the sweet and sour sauce. Serve with rice and enjoy.

Air Fryer
Stuffed Chicken Breast

Ingredients

- 2 chicken breasts
- 2 slices Cheddar cheese
- 2 slices ham
- 2 large slices of tomato
- ½ teaspoon garlic powder
- ½ teaspoon Italian seasoning
- 1 tablespoon light olive oil
- 2 wooden toothpicks

SERVES 2

390
calories
per serving

Method

Cut a horizontal pocket into each chicken breast without cutting the whole way through. In a bowl, mix together the oil, Italian seasoning and garlic powder then add the chicken and coat it in the mixture. Stuff the pocket you made with a slice of ham, cheese and tomato. Seal it closed using a wooden toothpick. Place the chicken into the air fryer and cook at 180C/360F for around 20 minutes or until it is completely cooked through. You can use a meat thermometer for this and if it's not sufficiently done, cook it for longer until it is thoroughly cooked.

Air Fryer Meat Loaf

Ingredients

450g (1lb) beef mince,
(pork or turkey can also be used)

75g (3oz) breadcrumbs

1 egg

1 tablespoon tomato purée (paste)

1 teaspoon mixed herbs

1 teaspoon Worcestershire sauce

Sea salt

Freshly ground black pepper

**SERVES
4**

298
calories
per serving

Method

Place all of the ingredients into a large bowl and mix them well. Transfer the meat to a loaf tin which fits into your air fryer. Place it in the air fryer and cook at 190C/380F for 25 minutes then check to see if it is done. Cook for another 5-7 minutes if you need to until it is completely cooked. Serve and enjoy.

Air Fryer Steak & Garlic Butter

Ingredients

- 25g (1oz) butter
- 2 rump steaks (approx. 250g/8oz)
- 2 cloves of garlic, peeled and chopped
- Small bunch of fresh parsley, finely chopped
- Sea salt
- Freshly ground black pepper

SERVES 2

386 calories per serving

Method

Preheat the air fryer to 200C/400F. In a small bowl, mix together the butter, garlic and parsley. Season the steaks with salt and pepper. Transfer them to the basket of the air fryer, with enough space between them to ensure even cooking. Cook the steaks for 6 minutes then turn them over and continue cooking for 4 minutes then check if they are cooked the way you like them. Continue cooking for another 2-3 minutes if you like them well done. Serve immediately with a dollop of garlic butter on top. Enjoy.

Air Fryer
Chicken & Broccoli

Ingredients

- 2 breasts of chicken, cut into chunks
- ¼ of a broccoli head, chopped
- 2 spring onions (scallions), chopped
- 2 tablespoons olive oil
- 1 teaspoon garlic powder
- 1 teaspoon paprika
- Sea salt
- Freshly ground black pepper

SERVES 2

352 calories per serving

Method

In a small bowl, mix together the olive oil, garlic powder and paprika. Place the chopped chicken into a bowl and the broccoli to a separate bowl. Pour half the oil mixture over the chicken and half over the broccoli and coat them well. Place the chicken in the air fryer basket and cook at 190C/380F for 10 minutes. Add the broccoli to the air fryer basket and stir well. Cook for around 10 minutes, or until the chicken is cooked through and the broccoli has softened. Scatter the spring onions (scallions) on top. Serve with rice, potatoes, pasta or a salad.

Air Fryer
Pork Tenderloin

Ingredients

- 350g (12oz) pork tenderloin
- 2 teaspoons smooth mustard
- 1 teaspoon garlic powder
- Sea salt
- Freshly ground black pepper

SERVES 2

316
calories
per serving

Method

Preheat the air fryer to 190C/380F. In a small bowl, mix together the mustard, garlic powder and a sprinkle of salt and pepper. Spread the mustard mixture over the pork. Grease the basket of the air fryer and add the tenderloin. Cook for around 20 minutes then use a meat thermometer to check if it is completely cooked. Allow it to stand for a few minutes before serving.

Air Fryer Lemon Cod

Ingredients

- 4 cod fillets (approx. 125g each)
- 2 tablespoons olive oil
- Juice of ½ lemon
- Small handful of fresh parsley or dill, chopped
- Sea salt
- Freshly ground black pepper
- Lemon slices for garnish

SERVES 4

180
calories
per serving

Method

Place the oil into a bowl and add in the lemon juice. Coat the fish with the oil and season with salt and pepper. Place the cod fillets into the air fryer in a single layer. Cook at 200C/400F for 10 minutes. Check that the fish is completely opaque and cooked through. Serve with a slice of lemon and a sprinkle of parsley or dill. Enjoy with fries or new potatoes and salad.

SIDES
& SNACKS

Air Fryer
Sweet Potato Fries

Ingredients

2 medium sweet potatoes, peeled

2 teaspoons vegetable oil

½ teaspoon sea salt

¼ teaspoon garlic powder

¼ teaspoon paprika

**SERVES
2**

173
calories
per serving

Method

Chop the sweet potatoes into even ½ cm (¼ inch) chips sticks. Preheat the air fryer to 200C/400F. Place all of ingredients into a large bowl and toss the fries in the oil and seasoning mixture. Scatter the fries out evenly in the basket of the air fryer. Depending on the size of your air fryer, you may wish to cook your fries in 2 batches and keep them warm. Place the sweet potato into the air fryer and cook for 6 minutes then turn them over and cook for another 6 minutes. Serve hot with your favourite dip.

Air Fryer Turmeric Falafels

Ingredients

- 400g (14oz) tin chickpeas, drained
- 2 cloves of garlic, peeled and roughly chopped
- 2 teaspoons turmeric
- Zest of ½ lemon
- ½ small onion, peeled and chopped
- ½ teaspoon ground coriander (cilantro)
- ½ teaspoon sea salt
- ½ teaspoon black pepper
- 2 tablespoons water (or more if needed)
- A handful of fresh coriander (cilantro)

MAKES 8

46 calories per serving

Method

Preheat the air fryer to 200°C.Place all the ingredients for the falafels into a food processor and blitz until the mixture sticks together. You can add an extra tablespoon of water to the mixture if it seems too dry. Shape the mixture into 8 balls. Spray a little vegetable oil into the basket of the air fryer and lay the falafels out in a single layer. Cook at 200C/400F for around 15 minutes or until crisp and golden.

Air Fryer Onion Bhajis

Ingredients

- 125g (4oz) gram flour/chickpea (garbanzo) flour
- 2 large onions, peeled and thinly sliced
- 1 teaspoon ground coriander
- 1 teaspoon cumin
- ½ teaspoon turmeric
- ½ teaspoon chilli powder
- 2 teaspoons water
- Sea salt
- A few sprays of vegetable oil

SERVES 4

162
calories
per serving

Method

Place all the dry ingredients except the water, into a bowl and mix well. Using clean hands, squeeze the mixture together then let it sit for 30 minutes to let the moisture infuse. Add 2 teaspoons water and mix well. Preheat the air fryer to 200C/400F. Spoon some of the bhaji mixture in small bundles and lay it in the air fryer basket in one single layer. Spray with oil and cook for 5 minutes. Turn them and continue cooking for another 5-6 minutes or a little longer for extra crispness.

Air Fryer Crispy Onions

Ingredients

2 large onions, peeled, sliced and separated into rings

1 tablespoon vegetable oil

SERVES 2

142 calories per serving

Method

Preheat the air fryer to 160C/320F. Coat the onions in the oil and place them in the air fryer basket. Cook for 5 minutes, stir them and cook for another 5 minutes. Reduce the temperature to 120C/240F and cook for another 5 minutes or until they are crispy and golden. Crispy onions taste great on top of steak, chicken and burgers. You can cook them in batches ahead of time and warm them for a minute or two just before serving.

Air Fryer Keto Courgette Bites

Ingredients

2 large courgettes (zucchini), evenly sliced

½ teaspoon onion powder

½ teaspoon garlic powder

1 tablespoon vegetable oil

Sea salt

SERVES 4

57 calories per serving

Method

Place the oil, onion and garlic powder into a bowl and mix well. Add the courgette (zucchini) slices and coat them in the oil. Transfer them to the basket of the air fryer. Cook them at 200C/400F for 7 minutes then flip and shake them around. Continue cooking for 7-8 minutes or until crisp. Eat them on their own as a snack or add them to salads and meat dishes.

Air Fryer
Roast Vegetables

Ingredients

- 14 medium mushrooms, halved
- 2 carrots, peeled and chopped
- 1 small cauliflower, broken into florets
- 1 courgette (zucchini), sliced
- 1 red onion, cut into wedges
- 2 tablespoons light olive oil
- 1 tablespoon balsamic vinegar
- 1 mixed herbs or Herb de Provence
- 3 cloves of garlic, peeled and chopped
- Sea salt
- Freshly ground black pepper

SERVES 4

136 calories per serving

Method

Preheat the air fryer to 180C/360F. Place the oil, balsamic vinegar, herbs and garlic into a bowl and mix well. Add the vegetables to the bowl and coat them in the oil mixture. Transfer the vegetables to the air fryer and spread them out in a single layer. Cook them for 5 minutes then flip them over and continue cooking for another 5 minutes. Leave them a little longer if you want them crispier. Serve with meat, pasta and rice dishes.

Air Fryer Vegetable Fried Rice

Ingredients

- 100g (3½ oz) mixed frozen vegetables
- 2 packs of pre cooked rice
- 1 egg, beaten
- 1 tablespoon olive oil
- 2 teaspoons soy sauce
- Sea salt
- Freshly ground black pepper

SERVES 2

454 calories per serving

Method

Preheat the air fryer to 180C/360F. Pour the beaten egg into an oven proof bowl or air fryer tin and cook it for around 2 minutes. Using a fork, scramble the mixture and continue cooking for another minute or so. Place the rice, vegetables, olive oil and soy sauce into a bowl and mix well. Transfer it to the air fryer and cook for around 10 minutes, stirring half way through. Add in the scrambled egg and continue cooking for around 5 minutes or until the rice and vegetables are warmed through. Season with salt and pepper and extra soy sauce if you wish. Serve and enjoy.

Air Fryer
Mexican Sweet Potato

Ingredients

2 medium sweet potatoes, peeled and cubed

2 tablespoons avocado oil

2 cloves of garlic, peeled and chopped

2 teaspoons smoked paprika

2 teaspoons cumin

1 teaspoon onion powder

½ teaspoon chilli flakes

¼ teaspoon black pepper

Sea salt

Freshly ground black pepper

SERVES 2

271
calories
per serving

Method

Preheat the air fryer to 200C/400F. Place the spices and oil in a bowl and mix well. Coat the sweet potatoes in the seasoning. Transfer them to the air fryer and cook for 6 minutes then flip them over. Continue cooking for another 6 minutes or until crispy. Serve and enjoy.

Air Fried Tofu

Ingredients

- 300g (11oz) block of tofu, diced
- 2 teaspoons corn flour (corn starch)
- 1 teaspoon paprika
- Sea salt
- Freshly ground black pepper

SERVES 2

197 calories per serving

Method

Preheat the air fryer to 190C/380F. In a bowl, mix together the corn flour (corn starch) and paprika and coat the tofu in the mixture making sure it is dry beforehand. Place the tofu into the basket of the air fryer and cook for 5 minutes then flip it over. Continue cooking for another 5 minutes and flip it over again. Continue cooking for another 2-3 minutes and check to see if it is crisp and golden. You can add a little extra cooking time if you want it crispier. Serve it with dips, vegetables or rice dishes.

Air Fryer Kale Chips

Ingredients

- 250g (9oz) kale, roughly chopped and thick stalk removed

- 1 teaspoon Parmesan cheese, grated (shredded) optional

- 1/4 teaspoon sea salt

- 1/4 teaspoon freshly ground black pepper

- 1 tablespoon light olive oil

SERVES 4

52 calories per serving

Method

Place the salt, pepper, olive oil and Parmesan (if using) into a bowl and mix well. Toss the kale in the mixture making sure it is completely coated. Transfer the kale to the air fryer basket and cook at 140C/280F for around 5 minutes then shake it and continue cooking for 3 minutes. You may need to prevent the kale blowing around by using a little foil folded on top of the kale. Check to see if it's crispy and add another 1-2 minutes of cooking time if you need to. These are a great healthy snack. You can experiment with different seasonings like garlic powder, smoked paprika, curry powder or Mexican seasoning. It goes well with hummus and guacamole too.

Air Fryer
Corn-On-The-Cob

Ingredients

2 large corn, leaves removed and halved

25g (1oz) butter

Sea salt

Freshly ground black pepper

SERVES 2

177
calories
per serving

Method

Rub some of the butter onto the corn making sure they are completely covered. Place the 4 pieces into the air fryer and cook for 4 minutes. Flip them over and continue cooking for another 4 minutes. Serve with the remaining butter and season with salt and pepper. Serve and enjoy.

Air Fryer
Roast Broccoli

Ingredients

450g (1lb) broccoli, broken into florets

1 onion, peeled and chopped

1 tablespoon olive oil

2 tablespoons water

Sea salt

SERVES 4

77
calories
per serving

Method

Place the oil, onion, salt and pepper into a bowl and toss the broccoli florets in the ingredients. Transfer the broccoli to the basket of the air fryer. Put the water into the bottom tray to prevent it drying out. Cook on 200C/400F for 4 minutes. Flip the broccoli over and continue cooking for around 3 minutes or until it is cooked to your liking. Serve and enjoy.

Air Fryer
Roast Potatoes

Ingredients

1kg (2.25lb) potatoes, peeled

2 tablespoons avocado oil

Sea salt

Black pepper

SERVES 2

246 calories per serving

Method

Chop the potatoes into quarters, or smaller if the potatoes are large. Place them into a saucepan of cold water, bring them to the boil and cook for 5 minutes. Drain them and toss them around to roughen the edges. Place them into a bowl and coat them well in the oil. Transfer them to the air fryer and cook at 200C/400F for 15 minutes then turn them and cook for another 10 minutes or until the potatoes are crisp. Season with salt and pepper. Roast potatoes can be batch cooked and frozen until you need them.

Air Fryer
Baked Potatoes

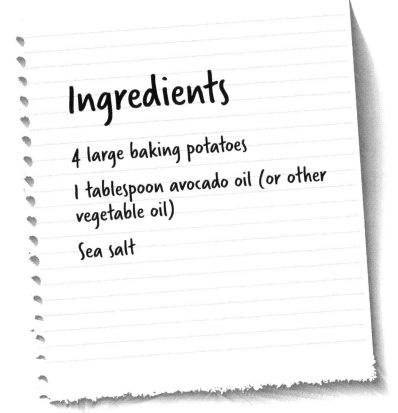

Ingredients

- 4 large baking potatoes
- 1 tablespoon avocado oil (or other vegetable oil)
- Sea salt

SERVES 4

243 calories per serving

Method

Rub the oil into the potatoes and season them with some salt. Transfer them to the air fryer and cook at 200C/400F for 35 minutes. Test the firmness using a skewer or knife and if they are not soft on the inside cook them for 2 minute increments until they are. They can be served with butter or your favourite topping. Also see recipe for loaded potato skins.

Air Fryer Cheesy Garlic Bread

Ingredients

75g (3oz) mozzarella cheese, grated (shredded)

25g (1oz) butter, softened

3 cloves of garlic, crushed

1 small French baguette, sliced

SERVES 4

187
calories
per serving

Method

Preheat the air fryer to 160C/320F. In a small bowl, mix together the butter with the crushed garlic. Spread some garlic butter onto one side of each slice of bread and sprinkle some cheese on top. Place the slices onto the shelves in the air fryer and make sure a drip tray or piece of foil is at the bottom to catch any cheesy drips. Cook for 2 minutes and if the cheese has not melted enough, continue cooking until it is done.

Air Fryer
Brussels Sprouts

Ingredients

18 medium Brussels sprouts, halved

1 teaspoon garlic powder

½ teaspoon salt

A few sprays of vegetable oil

DRESSING

1 teaspoon maple syrup

2 teaspoons balsamic vinegar

SERVES 2

47
calories
per serving

Method

Preheat the air fryer to 180C/360F. Place the oil, garlic and salt into a bowl and toss the sprouts in the mixture. Place the sprouts in the basket of the air fryer and cook for 10 minutes. In a bowl mix together the maple syrup and balsamic vinegar. Add the sprouts to dressing and serve as an accompaniment to chicken and meat dishes.

Air Fryer Vegetable Chips

Ingredients

- 2 beetroot, peeled and thinly sliced
- 2 carrots, peeled and thinly sliced
- 1 parsnip, peeled and thinly sliced
- 1 tablespoon vegetable oil
- 1/2 teaspoon dried mixed herbs
- 1/4 teaspoon garlic powder
- Sea salt
- Freshly ground black pepper

SERVES 4

71 calories per serving

Method

You can use a mandolin to chop the vegetables thinly or even a peeler. Scatter the vegetables onto a piece of kitchen paper to dry them off. Place the oil, herbs and garlic powder into a bowl and mix well. Add the vegetables and coat them in the mixture. Season with salt and pepper. Scatter the vegetable chips into the basket of the air fryer. Cook at 200C/400F for around 3 minutes. Toss them around and continue cooking for around another 3 minutes. Check if they are crisp and continue cooking at 1 minute intervals until they are crispy and done to your liking.

Air Fryer
Homemade Tortilla Chips

Ingredients

4 flour tortillas, quartered

2 teaspoons vegetable oil

Sea salt

**SERVES
2**

285
calories
per serving

Method

Spray each piece of tortilla with a little oil and season with salt. Spread them out in a single layer in the air fryer. You can cook them in batches if you haven't much space. Cook the tortillas at 180C/360F for around 5 minutes then turn them over and continue cooking for around 3 minutes. Check that they are crispy then remove them from the air fryer. Serve with guacamole and salsa.

Air Fryer Croutons

Ingredients

50g (2oz) butter, melted

4 slices of white bread, cubed

½ teaspoon dried parsley

¼ teaspoon sea salt

**SERVES
4**

172
calories
per serving

Method

Preheat the air fryer to 200C/400F. Place the melted butter, sea salt and parsley into a bowl. Add the bread cubes, toss them in the butter and allow them to absorb it. Place the bread into the basket of the air fryer and cook it for 3 minutes. Toss them and continue cooking for 2-3 minutes or until they are golden. Depending on the thickness of the bread you may need to adjust your cooking time. Remove them and store until ready to serve, with soups or salads.

DESSERTS

Air Fryer Carrot Cake & Cream Cheese Frosting

Ingredients

- 200g (7oz) self raising flour
- 175g (6oz) grated (shredded) carrots
- 150g (5oz) butter
- 150g (5oz) demerara sugar
- 50g (2oz) sultanas
- 2 eggs, beaten
- Zest and juice of 1 orange
- 1 teaspoon ground cinnamon
- ½ teaspoon ground nutmeg
- 50g (2oz) walnuts, chopped, for garnish

FOR THE ICING:

- 150g (5oz) icing sugar
- 50g (2oz) butter
- 50g (2oz) low fat cream cheese

SERVES 10

382 calories per serving

Method

Preheat the air fryer to 170C/340F. Place the butter and sugar into a bowl and combine them until creamy. Gradually pour in the beaten eggs whilst mixing together until smooth. Gradually add in the flour and combine it well. Next add in the carrots, sultanas, orange zest and juice and mix together until it's all combined. Grease a baking tin with a little butter and then pour in the cake mixture. Transfer it to the air fryer and cook for 25 minutes. Using a metal skewer, test the middle of the cake to see if it is cooked. If the skewer comes out clean it is done. If not allow another few minutes until it is completely cooked. Allow the carrot cake to cook before removing it from the tin.

FOR THE FROSTING:

Place the icing sugar and butter into a bowl and beat it until smooth. Add in the soft cheese and stir until it is creamy. Spread the cream onto the carrot cake. Sprinkle the chopped walnuts on top.

Air Fryer Chocolate Mug Cakes

Ingredients

- 50g (2oz) plain (all-purpose) flour
- 4 tablespoons 100% cocoa powder
- 6 tablespoons sugar
- 2 tablespoons chocolate chips
- 1 teaspoon vanilla extract
- 1 teaspoon baking powder
- 100mls (4fl oz) whole milk
- 4 tablespoons vegetable oil

SERVES 4

339 calories per serving

Method

Place the flour, sugar, baking powder, cocoa powder, milk, vegetable oil and vanilla extract into a bowl and mix well. Add in the chocolate chips and combine the mixture. Lightly grease 4 mugs (or ramekin dish) with a spray of vegetable oil. Spoon some chocolate mixture into each of the mugs. Transfer them to the air fryer and cook at 180C/360F and cook for 10-11 minutes or until they have risen nicely. Serve them with a dollop or cream and enjoy!

Air Fryer Banana & Oat Cookies

Ingredients

- 175g (5oz) rolled oats
- 50g (2oz) raisins
- 2 medium bananas, peeled

MAKES 10

96
calories
per serving

Method

Place the bananas into a bowl and mash them to a pulp. Add in the oats and raisins and combine them. Divide the mixture into 10 and shape them into rounds. Spray the air fryer basket with oil. Lay the cookies into the basket in a single layer, bearing in mind you may want to do it in batches. Cook them at 160C/320F. Remove the cookies and allow them to cool. Enjoy!

Air Fryer Brownies

Ingredients

- 175g (6oz) milk chocolate chips
- 125g (4oz) plain (all-purpose) flour
- 75g (3oz) butter
- 75g (3oz) sugar
- 2 eggs
- 2 tablespoons water
- ½ teaspoon baking powder
- ¼ teaspoon salt
- 1 teaspoon vanilla extract

MAKES 9

268 calories per serving

Method

Preheat the air fryer to 160C/320F. Line a cake tin, which is the right size for your air fryer, with parchment paper. Place the butter and half the chocolate chips into a bowl and microwave them until they have melted. Stir well, and then let it cool slightly. Mix in the sugar, eggs, water and vanilla extract. Stir in the flour, baking soda, salt and the rest of the chocolate chips. Pour the mixture into the lined cake tin. Transfer it to the air fryer and cook for around 40 minutes. Insert a thin skewer or tooth pick and if it comes out clean it is cooked. Return it for a few more minutes of cooking time if you need to. For variety you can try adding in chopped walnuts, caramel to the cake mix before cooking, or swap the water for coffee for a mocha brownie. Try serving with your favourite ice cream, it's delicious!

Air Fryer Baked Pineapple & Ice Cream

Ingredients

- 25g (1oz) butter, melted
- 25g (1oz) brown sugar (or honey)
- 8 slices of tinned pineapple (or fresh if you prefer)
- 4 scoops of vanilla ice cream
- ½ teaspoon cinnamon

SERVES 4

191 calories per serving

Method

Preheat the air fryer to 190C/380F. Place the butter, sugar and cinnamon into a bowl and mix well. Add the pineapple and coat it in the mixture. Transfer it to the air fryer and lay it out in a single layer. Cook for 4 minutes then turn it over and cook for another 4 minutes. Serve hot with a scoop of ice cream.

Air Fryer Blueberry Muffins

Ingredients

- 125g (4oz) plain flour (all purpose flour)
- 75g (3oz) sugar
- 75g (3oz) blueberries
- 1 egg
- 2 tablespoons olive oil
- 80mls (3fl oz) whole milk
- ½ teaspoon vanilla extract
- ½ teaspoon baking powder

MAKES 6

187 calories per serving

Method

For this recipe you will need either a silicon 6 muffin tray or a non stick 6 muffin tray which fits inside your air fryer. Grease the muffin tin with oil. Place the milk, sugar, vanilla, olive oil and egg into a bowl and mix thoroughly. Gradually add in the flour, baking powder, sugar and mix to a smooth batter. Add in all but a few blueberries which will go on top of the muffin. Spoon the muffin mixture into the tray cups. Place some blueberries on top of each one. Transfer it to the air fryer and cook at 150C/300F for around 20 minutes or until the muffins have risen and are golden.

Air Fryer
Banana Chips

Ingredients

2 bananas, peeled

1 teaspoon olive oil

½ teaspoon cinnamon

**SERVES
2**

103
calories
per serving

Method

Chop the banana into ½ cm (¼ inch) slices. Put the olive oil and cinnamon into a bowl and mix well. Add the banana and coat it in the mixture. Lay the banana slices into the air fryer in one single layer. Cook at 180C/360F for 8-9 minutes or until crispy and golden.

Air Fryer
Dried Apple Slices

Ingredients

2 apples

½ teaspoon cinnamon

SERVES
2

52
calories
per serving

Method

Preheat the air fryer to 180C/360F. Very thinly slice the apple and discard the core. Sprinkle with cinnamon and lay the apple slices in single layers on the shelves of the air fryer. Cook for 5 minutes, turn them over and continue cooking for another 5 minutes. Delicious served cold as a healthy snack or warm with ice cream.

You may also be interested in other titles by
Erin Rose Publishing
which are available in both paperback and ebook.

 Quick Start Guides

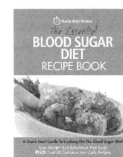

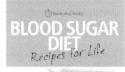

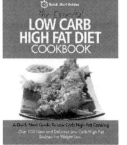

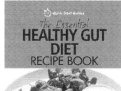

The Essential
HEALTHY GUT DIET
RECIPE BOOK

A Quick Start Guide To Improving Your
Digestion, Health And Wellbeing
PLUS over 80 Delicious Gut-Friendly Recipes

The Essential
Low FODMAP Diet
COOKBOOK

A Quick Start Guide To Relieving
the Symptoms of IBS Through Diet
Improve Your Digestion, Health and Wellbeing
PLUS over 75 IBS-Friendly Recipes

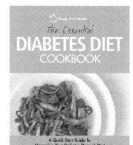

The Essential
DIABETES DIET
COOKBOOK

A Quick Start Guide To
Managing Your Diabetes Through Diet
PLUS over 100 Patients-Friendly Recipes

The
ALKALINE DIET
SOLUTION

A Quick Start Guide To The Alkaline Diet
Lose Weight, Improve Your Health and Feel Great
PLUS over 90 Alkaline Friendly Recipes

The Essential
THYROID DIET
RECIPE BOOK

A Quick Start Guide To Healing Your Thyroid
Through Diet, Lose Weight And Feel Great
With Delicious Thyroid Friendly Recipes

The Essential
SIRT FOOD
DIET RECIPE BOOK

A Quick Start Guide to Cooking on the SIRT Food Diet
Over 100 Easy and Delicious Recipes to Burn Fat,
Lose Weight, Get Lean and Feel Great!

What Can I Eat
ON A
DAIRY FREE
DIET

A Quick Start Guide To Quitting Dairy and Lactose
Raise Weight, Improve Your Health and Energy
PLUS 100 Delicious Dairy-Free Recipes

LOWER
CHOLESTEROL
DIET

A Quick Start Guide To Lower Cholesterol
Improve Your Health and Feel Great
PLUS over 100 Delicious Cholesterol-Lowering Recipes

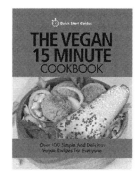

THE VEGAN
15 MINUTE
COOKBOOK

Over 100 Simple And Delicious
Vegan Recipes For Everyone

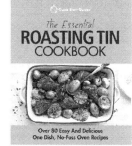

The Essential
ROASTING TIN
COOKBOOK

Over 80 Easy And Delicious
One Dish, No-Fuss Oven Recipes

Blood Sugar Diet
Diary

Daily Diary To Track Foods, Weight Loss
And Wellbeing On the Blood Sugar Diet

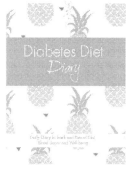

Diabetes Diet
Diary

Daily Diary to Track and Record Diet
Blood Sugar and Well-being

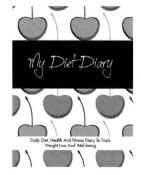

My Diet Diary

Daily Diet, Health And Fitness Diary To Track
Weight Loss And Well-being

Low FODMAP
Food Diary

Daily Diary to Track Foods And Symptoms
To Ease IBS And Digestive Disorders

Sugar-Free Diet
Diary

Daily Diary For Quitting Sugar,
Losing Weight and Feeling Great

FOOD
Diary

Daily Diary To Track Diet And Symptoms
To Beat Food Intolerances And Digestive Disorders

Printed in Great Britain
by Amazon

41445194R10057